Title:
VERMICOMPOSTING
(Worm Farming)

Subtitle
All You Need to Know About Compost Farming, Vermiculture, and Making Worm Bins for Beginners.

Vermicomposting

(Worm Farming)

All You Need to Know About Compost Farming, Vermiculture, and Making Worm Bins for Beginners.

TABLE OF CONTENT

Introduction

Did you know that, in some conditions, it is possible to turn food waste into valuable gold? The theme of vermicomposting is not alchemy; rather, it is vermicomposting as a decomposition procedure, which is the subject of this article.

Natural, ecologically friendly, and incredibly successful way of making nutrient-dense compost for use in gardening, vermicomposting (also known as worm farming) is becoming increasingly popular. Using worm composting, you may improve the overall quality of your compost by taking advantage of the natural digestive process. Wolves that are healthy, fed, and pooping are good to your garden in addition to offering an almost limitless supply of high-quality fertilizer.

What Is A Worm Farm?

It is critical that you grasp the operation of worm farming before you begin. It is important to note that at its foundation, worm farming is an environmentally beneficial means of producing nutrient-dense compost. Compared to other composting procedures, this compost is an ideal alternative for home gardening because it is much easier to obtain and less expensive than other composting techniques.

traditionally, gardeners wishing to use compost have been had to do one of two things: either wait for it to deteriorate naturally – which can be stinky (and time-consuming!) – or pay money on fertilizer that has been made elsewhere, which can quickly add up in price (especially for those who like to do a lot of gardening).

Why Should You Start Raising Worms?

The numerous benefits that growing worms can give may come as a pleasant surprise to you when you read about them. Individuals who are willing to put in the effort to cultivate weeds can reap significant rewards, regardless of whether their primary concerns are environmental, monetary, or horticultural in character. Despite the fact that worm farming has a number of additional advantages, our readers have identified the following as the four most significant advantages:

1. Valuable Teaching Opportunities

Additional benefits include the fact that vermicomposting is a wonderful activity that you may introduce your child to. Although most children are able to pick up the game quickly because it is simple to understand, it does require a level of responsibility that will be invaluable in the long term. If you can spare a few minutes every day to complete the vermicomposting process, you will have the best results. Depending on your preferences, caring for a pet might be an excellent alternative (or addition) to teaching your child responsibility.

As an added advantage, vermicomposting teaches your child about the necessity of conservation, which is a valuable life lesson. Growing worms provides them with an enjoyable and rewarding approach to learn about gardening since they understand the worms' language. Consider the following: many youngsters already play in the dirt, so why not turn it into a worthwhile activity?

2. Decreased Household Waste

On a daily basis, we generate large amounts of garbage in our residences. A typical day would include everything from banana peels to old newspapers piling up to create a substantial amount of garbage that would be thrown away. Americans generate approximately 67 million tons of organic waste each year, with less than a third of that waste getting composted, according to estimates. Another explanation for this tendency is that many Americans believe composting is either too complicated or not worth their time and effort, which is one of the causes for this belief.

Vermicomposting is by far one of the most successful techniques of reducing your household's environmental impact, whether you wish to minimize your household's environmental impact or simply love the concept of repurposing waste in a useful way.

It is also possible to use not just organic trash but also non-organic waste in this process. Newspapers and cardboard are examples of the forms of paper waste that can be composted as part of the process of decomposition.

3. Unlimited Supply of "Black Gold"

Gardeners who have been in the hobby for a long time are well aware that fertilizer is one of the most expensive products in the home gardening budget. The costs of growing your own fruits and vegetables can be prohibitively high; nevertheless, the rewards (both in terms of enjoyment and in terms of financial savings) almost always outweigh the costs. Consider the alternative: what if you had the power to manufacture all of the fertilizer you needed for free? Yes, isn't it true that having a garden would make gardening even more enjoyable?

Because of this, the term "black gold" is frequently used to characterize the compost created by vermicomposting. Because of the incredible nutrient density of the material, it has the capacity to change even the most barren soil (such as the type of soil you'll find in your backyard) into good gardening soil. Use of this "black gold" on a consistent basis will save you hundreds, if not thousands, of dollars in fertilizer costs! This strategy has numerous advantages, including the ability to save time, money, and the environment.

4. Good Conversation Starter.

Worm farms are becoming increasingly popular in a variety of geographical locations throughout the world. However, it is still a relatively new concept in many regions of the United States, particularly in the southern states, where it is particularly prevalent. You can find the subject of vermicomposting to be a fascinating and profitable addition to your conversation if gardening is something you enjoy discussing with your friends.

Benefits of Worm Castings

On the earth, worm castings are the most efficient source of compost production. Furthermore, in addition to being manufactured in accordance with a fully organic process, they include the optimal balance of nitrogen, phosphates and potassium, as well as all of the other plant nutrients that your garden requires in order to thrive. The Red Wiggler worm is the most effective worm for vermicomposting applications by a long shot, and it is the most widely distributed worm in the world.

Wrongly identified worm shells are a byproduct of the digestive process that worms go through throughout their life cycle. In the course of its natural decay, the material naturally mixes into the soil of the worm farm, resulting in the manufacture of the highly sought after fertilizer that is created.

It is not required to be concerned that gathering worm castings is interfering with the natural process in order to get the benefits. In fact, according to several studies, worms do not genuinely thrive in their own castings, so every time you harvest new fertilizer for your garden, you will be doing them a favor.

There are a number of other advantages to using worm castings, including the following:

☐ Alternative fertilizer that is completely non-toxic and made from organic materials
☐ It has a milder odor than other fertilizers.
☐ Fertilizer created from worm casings can have up to five times the nitrogen content, seven times the potassium, and 1.5 times the calcium of normal soil, according to recent studies.

Difficult Level Of Worm Farming

In a nutshell, the answer is no! Worm farming is a straightforward method that everyone can learn. We recommend that you teach your children how to do it because it is a valuable skill that can be learnt by even very young children and that adults can entirely control. Following the simple procedures below, a worm farm can be constructed in a couple of minutes:

1. **Build or buy a container: In order to house the farm, the first step is to acquire or construct a container (which is typically constructed of wood or plastic). While it is possible to construct your own container, commercially manufactured containers are more dependable over time and are guaranteed not to interfere with the normal activities of the worm farm.**

2.   Fill the container with appropriate bedding: Before adding the worms, line the container with moist newspaper (or equivalent appropriate bedding), and then fill the container with ordinary soil, either purchased or collected from your backyard. The dirt in the container should be moist enough to allow it to remain loosely packed, but not so wet that the worms perish from drowning. Egg shells can also be used to improve the soil's fertility (if you have them).

3.   Red Wigglers should be used to populate the farm: This step is simple: simply insert the worms in the container you've chosen. Never be concerned about introducing an excessive number (or a deficient number) of worms into your farm; worms will quickly self-regulate their population.

4.   Provide compostable material: Compostable materials might range from kitchen waste to lawn mowing leftovers, among other things. Any organic matter that decomposes naturally can be used on the farm, according to a simple guideline. It is important to note that there are some types of compost that should not be used in a worm farm. Dairy products, meats, citrus fruits, spicy meals, fats, oils, and foods that have been overly processed are examples of these foods.

5.   **Maintain and harvest the farm: It is critical to prevent overfeeding your worms, but it is also important to remember that they are ravenous eaters. Due to the fact that Red Wigglers consume nearly half of their body weight every 24 hours, you should be able to feed your worms new food on a daily basis (a fantastic chore for children!). Always remember to cut the meal into the tiniest pieces possible before serving it to your guests. Keep dairy and meat products away from the farm as well. These are more harder for the worms to consume and have a considerably stronger stench than the rest of the food.**

Tools Required To Start Worm Farming

A terrific choice, vermicomposting involves little initial investment and produces significant returns in a relatively short period of time.

Worm Composting Bin

In theory, you could use any container as a worm composting bin; nevertheless, some containers perform substantially better than others when it comes to worm composting performance. Utilizing containers that have been commercially built makes it much easier to maintain additional levels of your farm, and they will be significantly more reliable than anything you build yourself. Worm bins, which are specifically intended to meet the environmental concerns related with worm farming, are available for purchase in our online shop and may be found here.

Live Red Wiggler Composting Worms

As previously stated, not all worms are suitable for use in vermicomposting. Red Wigglers are by far the best choice since they produce the optimal combination of nutrients for gardening. While it is unlikely that you will be able to find Red Wigglers in your backyard on their own, they are incredibly affordable and can be purchased from our website at any time. Alternatively, you can purchase the critters required to continue manufacturing your own fertilizer for the price of a bag of fertilizer in perpetuity.

Worm Composting Accessories (Optional)

As far as necessary components are concerned, you will be able to get by with just a bin, some worms, and the fundamental ingredients that your worms will consume. The good news is that there are a lot of optional additions that make worm farming easier and can increase your crop (effectively paying for themselves over time) (effectively paying for themselves over time). It eliminates mistakes and saves you money in the long run when you have the instruments you need to ensure that your farm has the proper temperature, moisture, and pH.

Step 1: Choose Your New Worm Bin

Surprise! When starting a home bin, one of the first things you'll need is, well, a bin. There are various types of commercial bins available on the market, including:

☐ Worm Wigwam (warning: higly expensive)
☐ Worm Factory 360
☐ Can o' Worms
☐ The Urban Worm Bag

Additionally, there are some less expensive alternatives, such as a 10-to-18-gallon Rubbermaid bin or a basic 5-gallon bucket, both of which will require holes to be punched in the top 6 inches of either the sides or the lids of your new bin to allow it to breathe, as well as more expensive solutions.

If you want to keep the contents contained in the bin, you can also use a screen material as part (or the full) of the lid.

For the sake of simplicity, we'll go with the Rubbermaid option and my personal favorite (for obvious reasons), the Urban Worm Bag, rather than any of the other options on the market right now. Each has its own set of benefits and drawbacks, which are as follows:

Rubbermaid Bin

Pros

☐ Portable
☐ Cheap
☐ Decent surface area available

Cons

☐ Requires modification

☐ Castings are difficult to harvest
☐ Poor moisture control

Urban Worm Bag

Pros

☐ Zipper top makes feeding easy
☐ Castings are easy to harvest
☐ Breathable, maintains excellent aerobic conditions
☐ Free shipping and a lifetime warranty

Cons

☐ Can dry out in arid climates
☐ Somewhat more expensive.

Step 2: Make the Worm Bin a Home by adding bedding.

Following the acquisition of the bin, the following step is to clean it up a bit before beginning to load it with your bedding. The most efficient method of getting a new worm bin up and going is to take part of the contents from an existing bin. For the simple reason that if you are not cheating, you are not putting up any effort!

Incorporating an already-existing friendly habitat heavily populated with bacteria into your worm bin is a quick and simple way to make your worm house into a worm home without requiring any additional equipment. I believe you could cut your timeline by at least ten days, if not more, if you move more swiftly.

It won't take much work, on the other hand. If you have enough existing vermicompost, you should be able to replace 25 percent of the planned volume of bedding with it and fill the remaining 75 percent with new bedding; however, this will depend on the amount of bedding you were planning to start with.

Horse dung, on the other hand, has a number of disadvantages. It's typical to find rocks, weeds, rope, and other odd materials in horse feces collected from a field rather than a stall if you're utilizing dung collected from the field rather than from the stall. If you're utilizing dung that has been gathered from a stall, you're unlikely to come across anything like that.

It's possible that such pebbles will cause harm to your machinery and cause it to malfunction if you're digesting manure using a chipper shredder or grinder of some sort. A horse's intestines can also be penetrated by weed seeds that survive in aged horse manure that has not been thoroughly precomposted before being applied to a field or pasture.

I'd recommend putting enough horse manure in your bin to produce an 8-inch layer, then saturating that layer with water as needed until it has the consistency of a moist sponge...not dripping wet, but not fully dry either.

If you are unable to obtain any horse dung, I propose that you collect as much paper, newsprint, and corrugated cardboard as you possibly can to use as a substitute. Then immerse it in a sufficient amount of water for 24 hours after it has been shredded.

Watering paper products with a single sprinkle of water will not be enough to remove the toxins. The need to allow them to attain peak saturation cannot be overstated. To achieve the "damp sponge" effect, wring out your soaked paper and cardboard bedding after it has been soaking for 24 hours and dispose of it in your garbage disposal unit after it has been soaked for 24 hours.

Following that, there is a brief "do anything you want" sentence that appears to be an afterthought at first glance. As I reflect on my own personal experience, the more I know that it's critical if you're starting from scratch and don't have any past living material, such as horse manure or vermicompost, to include a live material source.

Due of the limitations of your ability to import an ecosystem, you will need to do your best efforts to imitate one by adding little amounts of the following materials in your bin with your bedding:

☐ Dead or composted leaves
☐ Soil
☐ Anything you wouldn't mind finding in your garden, basically
☐ A small amount of sand or limestone

A diversified, heterogeneous mixture of distinct substances with varying textures and physical qualities, as well as varying states and rates of breakdown, is produced as a result.

It is much less likely that you will make a mistake if you deliberately aim for "all of the above" while designing your worm home.

Step 3: Get the Microbes Blooming.

After all is said and done, we have constructed a safe and cozy home for your worms, but it is not quite ready for occupancy just yet. For starters, you should add some worm meal that will dissolve quite quickly in order to get the microbial party started right away.

It is sufficient to use a single banana peel or apple core for this purpose. Considering a microbe population to be analogous to a fire, the banana peel is one of the beginning logs that will help things get started in the proper direction for the most part.

Probably, you're thinking to yourself, "Wait a minute. What?" Using my recycling bin as a starting point, I'm asking myself, "Why am I putting food in my compost bin when I don't even have worms?"

I'm well aware of the circumstances. We're on the right track, thank you.

Step 4: Order Your Worms

You can purchase a pound of Red Wigglers or European Nightcrawlers from the Urban Worm Company or look for a trustworthy provider in your area that can give you with these worms.

It is critical to understand the following: To avoid worms being left in post office warehouses over the weekend, worm suppliers typically ship only on Mondays or Tuesdays, according to industry standards.

The cutoff period for a Monday shipment is also usually the Friday or Saturday before the shipment is to be delivered. That is to say, if you order worms on Monday and they are not delivered until the following Monday, you should expect to wait until the following Monday.

Step 5: Wait

If you are starting with a different bedding material than old horse manure or with an already-existing worm habitat such as vermicompost, this is really crucial to remember, and I cannot underline this point strongly enough.

Creating a microbe-rich environment will encourage the worms to hang out and consume their 5 little hearts' worth of food will be necessary to achieve this goal. No amount of wet paper and a fresh banana peel in a new plastic bin will be sufficient to solve the problem. It is vital to provide an environment conducive to the growth of microorganisms.

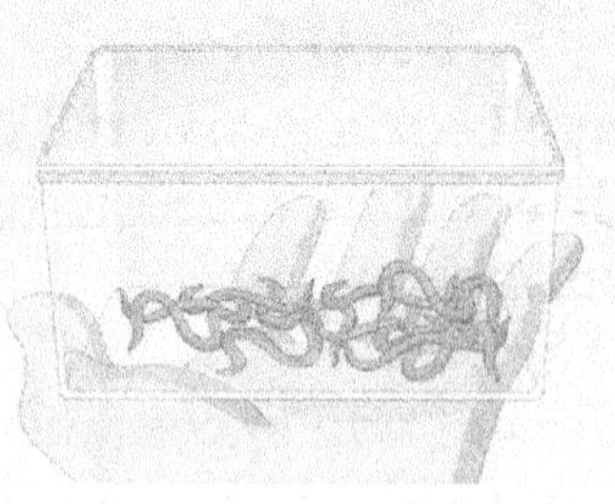

Step 6: The Worms Should Be Introduced to the Bin

It's time for your worms to make themselves at home! Toss them in the trash can and allow them to tuck themselves into their new bedding by placing your trash can (with the lid off) under a bright light for the first night in their new home. Worms do not like bright light and will seek refuge below the surface if they are subjected to an excessive amount of illumination.

This considerably reduces the possibility of a major jailbreak occurring within the first 24 hours following the indictment.

Step 7: Wait Again

As soon as the worms have been acclimated to their new home, you'll be ready to provide them with something to eat as quickly as possible. Please resist giving in to this temptation since, if you've done your job correctly, they will have plenty to eat at their new home if you don't.

Allow the bin a week to become acclimated to its new surroundings. While it is important to keep an eye on things, you should resist the desire to dig around to see how your worms are faring as well.

Step 8: Start Feeding (Slowly)

Depending on whether you started with a leafy or woody beginning medium, the surface of your worm environment may begin to look like the top of a pool table after a period of time as the worms work their way through the material on top of the surface. The usage of a layer of carpet, fabric, or cardboard on top of the food, bedding, and other supplies is very vital in these situations.

This appears to me to be a hint that it may be ready to begin feeding in earnest at this point in the game.

In the event that you do not develop the "felt" appearance on the surface, your discipline in not overfeeding up to this point should have paid off, and you should be fine to proceed from this point on.

However, keep in mind the following piece of advice: when it comes to feeding your worms, avoid falling into the trap of attempting to obtain some arbitrary percentage of worm weight. Vermicomposting expert Rhonda Sherman asserts that worms can devour 100-200 percent of their body weight in a single week, making her one of the world's foremost academic specialists on the subject.

Compared to the widely reported 50-100 percent a day statistic that has been thrown around, this is a significant improvement.

Because of this, once you've calculated how much to feed your worms, please review this guide on what to feed your worms. By ensuring that the quantity and quality of your food are both appropriate, you will be able to prevent many of the problems that new vermicomposters have during the early stages of their composting trip.

Step 9: Monitor Conditions

The ability to keep an eye on your worm bin without constantly disturbing your worms is a useful skill to have. Examine the following conditions and make any necessary adjustments to keep your worms happy and healthy as long as possible.

Alkalinity/ Acidity:

When it comes to the pH of your worm bin, it should be somewhat acidic, and it should remain that way unless you begin to overfeed the worms. The addition of lime, rock dust, and/or broken egg shells can help to restore balance to the pH of the water if it gets excessively acidic.

Temperature:

☐ The most convenient way to accomplish this is to store your bin inside, but if this is not possible, keep a shielded bin in the shade.
☐ Maintain a temperature range of roughly 60-80 degrees Fahrenheit inside the worm bin (15-27 degrees C)
☐ Consider purchasing an Urban Worm Thermometer to assist you in keeping track of the temperature.

Moisture:

☐ A worm bin should be kept damp, but not soaking wet, in order to maintain optimal performance. It's important to keep the humidity level between 60 and 70 percent at all times. The quantity I used to recommend was higher, but I recently published a blog entry outlining why I believe I was providing you terrible advise on worm bin moisture when I used to do so!)
☐ Your ability to maintain a moist environment is influenced by several factors, including the humidity and temperature of the surrounding environment, the type of bin or bed you're using, the type of food you feed them (most fruits and vegetables are 80-90 percent water), and the amount of food you feed them each day.
☐ Every now and again, take a handful of the contents of your rubbish bin and squeeze it in your hand to keep it from falling out. In order to tell if there is moisture in it, it should have the consistency of a damp sponge.

Extra Success Tips for Starting a Home Worm Bin

Air Matters

Worm composting is an aerobic process, and the quality of your castings (if you intend to use them, and especially if you intend to sell them) is directly proportional to the amount of time you spend maintaining highly aerobic conditions in your worm composting beds. If you intend to use your castings, the quality of your castings is directly proportional to the amount of time you spend maintaining highly aerobic conditions in your worm composting beds.

A larger bin and open air bin can include feedstocks such as small amounts of citrus or onions that would normally be avoided in a smaller bin and closed bin due to the acidity of the citrus or onions or the increased risk of mold in a smaller bin and closed bin.

Size Matters

You will be much better protected against your own mistakes if you have a larger, more expansive environment, because worms will be able to better escape the effects of overfeeding, overwatering, underwatering, and other mistakes that you will almost certainly make at the beginning of your gardening career. Keep in mind that the size of your worm bin serves as a safety net in the event that something terrible happens.

Practice Benign Neglect

When you first start off, it's difficult to keep your worms from assaulting you. And I can almost guarantee that your inquisitiveness will get the better of you at some point in the future. Fact: The scientific name for the red wiggler is eisenia fetida, with the "fetida" component referring to the foul-smelling mucous that red wigglers can exude when they are agitated or otherwise upset. The fact that I've never noticed anything offensive on them notwithstanding, it is widely known that mites may attack worms when they are under duress.

If you have mites in your garbage can, it is advisable not to remove them in this situation.

Don't Feed Every Day

They will be alright with a feeding every few days, and if you happen to go for a period of several weeks without feeding them, while it is not ideal, the negative consequences will be significantly less severe than those that will occur if you overfeed them.

Keep Adding Bedding

This does not imply that you should discontinue adding bedding to your worm bin, quite the contrary! The addition of bedding with each meal is not required, but bulking material such as shredded paper, cardboard, leaves, and potentially even wood chips should be added on a regular basis to ensure that the aquarium maintains aerobic conditions.

In contrast to underfeeding, which has a few mild side effects, "overbedding," on the other hand, has none that I am currently aware of. If you've already determined that you've added enough bedding, I practically guarantee that you'll be good with adding a bit extra later in the process.

Recognize the Signs of Success

You should be on the lookout for the following signs that you are doing something right with your worm bin:

☐ Worms aren't clumped together in the bin's corners.

☐ Worms that reproduce are content worms.

☐ However, there may be concentrations surrounding food that they're destroying.

☐ Worms aren't attempting to flee.

☐ You're probably doing it well if the worms are happy on or below the surface of your bed.

☐ The bin has a pleasant, earthy odor.

☐ Other creatures can be found.

☐ While not all non-worm organisms are useful to your worm bin, the fact that you've created a diverse habitat is a solid indication that you've done a good job of it.

Troubleshooting Worm Composting Issues

Being strict about the amount of food you throw in your garbage can will save you a lot of trouble in the future. Here's how to handle some of the most common worm bin issues:

☐ Fruit flies have made themselves at home in your worm bin: If you've ever had compost on your kitchen counter, you're well aware of how quickly a fruit fly infestation may spread throughout your home. The most important thing to keep in mind is that prevention is always preferable to cure. Make sure the food waste is thoroughly covered by the bedding, that it is cut up into little pieces, and that nothing is left to fester in the bin.

☐ It smells like your composter is deteriorating: As soon as you notice the scent emanating from your compost, rummage through the bedding to remove any food waste that appears to be decaying. It is possible that the worms will leave anything out to soften up even though they should be digesting everything they come across before it goes rotten and moldy. In the case of a fully matured fresh banana peel, it is improbable that they will swallow the entire thing before it begins to break down and become soft. The food will be processed more rapidly if the larger chunks are broken up into smaller pieces. It is also possible that a bad odor is indicative of the presence of a moisture problem. Because of the high humidity produced by big amounts of decaying rubbish, the bin will become soaked and a little too moist for the worms to survive happily. Add some dry cardboard and paper bedding to the mix to help restore the bedding's spongy moisture level and to help restore the bedding's balance.

☐ Worms are making their way out of the rubbish can: It is normal for a few worms to escape from a garbage can, but if you have a big number of escapees, you may be dealing with an environmental problem on your hands. Moisture, temperature, and possibly even pests will all be taken into consideration during this evaluation. If the bin is becoming too dry, it is necessary to add additional water. Extra bedding should be added if the bedding becomes too wet. Examine the bedding beneath the top layer for signs of bug larvae or other concerns that may exist.

☐ There's an infestation on the loose: Other critters may take pleasure in the moist, dark environment provided by the bin, even if it is merely for the purpose of laying their eggs there. Any insects, eggs, or hairy critters found in the bin should be removed and the castings should be collected outdoors. It's a great time of year to clean out the garbage can and get rid of any decomposing food or old bedding because the weather is nice. Restart the process with a clean slate and relocate the worms to their correct environment. If you have a rat infestation, you should use bungee cords or pebbles to secure the lid of the bin.